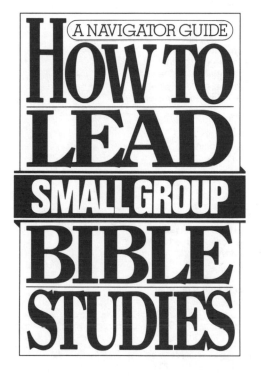

A NAVIGATOR GUIDE
HOW TO LEAD
SMALL GROUP
BIBLE STUDIES

NAVPRESS

A MINISTRY OF THE NAVIGATORS
P.O. Box 6000, Colorado Springs, CO 80934

The Navigators is an international Christian organization. Jesus Christ gave His followers the Great Commission to go and make disciples (Matthew 28:19). The aim of The Navigators is to help fulfill that commission by multiplying laborers for Christ in every nation.

NavPress is the publishing ministry of The Navigators. NavPress publications are tools to help Christians grow. Although publications alone cannot make disciples or change lives, they can help believers learn biblical discipleship, and apply what they learn to their lives and ministries.

Tenth printing, 1987

Printed in the United States of America

How to Lead Small Group Bible Studies is a revision of *Lead Out—A Guide for Leading Bible Discussion Groups* (1974).

79991

BIBLE STUDY MATERIALS FROM NAVPRESS

BIBLE STUDY SERIES

DESIGN FOR DISCIPLESHIP—seven books and leader's guide
EXPERIENCING GOD—three books
    Discovering God's Will
    Experiencing God's Attributes
    Experiencing God's Presence
GOD IN YOU—six books and leader's guide
GOD'S DESIGN FOR THE FAMILY—two books
LEARNING TO LIVE—six books
LIFECHANGE—studies of books of the Bible
STUDIES IN CHRISTIAN LIVING—nine books and leader's
    guide

TOPICAL BIBLE STUDIES

Becoming a Woman of Excellence
Celebrate the Seasons!
God, Man, and Jesus Christ
Homemaking
In His Name
On Holy Ground
Overcoming
Spiritual Fitness—also leader's guide
Think It Through
To Walk and Not Grow Weary

BIBLE STUDIES WITH COMPANION BOOKS

Essentials of Discipleship
The Freedom of Obedience
Friends and Friendship
Honesty, Morality, and Conscience
Marriage Takes More Than Love
The Power of Commitment
The Practice of Godliness
The Pursuit of Holiness
True Fellowship

RESOURCES

Explore the Bible Yourself
Leader's Guide for Evangelistic Bible Studies
The Navigator Bible Studies Handbook
Topical Memory System—available in KJV/NIV and
    NASB/RSV

CONTENTS

1. YOU CAN LEAD A SMALL GROUP BIBLE STUDY

Throughout the world today many committed Christians are witnessing the dynamic impact of small Bible study discussion groups. Sparked by their growing hunger for personal knowledge of God's word, these bands of eager learners are springing up everywhere. The intense fellowship, the personal interaction around the Scriptures, and the mutual commitment to application which is experienced in these groups is often unparalleled by other methods of spiritual development. Sometimes the vitality of Christian experience achieved becomes the springboard for a whole new spiritual awakening.

The idea of small groups isn't new. Almost two thousand years ago, the first followers of Jesus Christ met together in homes to hear the teachings of the apostles, to pray, to fellowship together, and to seek greater ministry outreach. The book of Acts records the impact and experiences these groups had in carrying out the Great Commission.

One person with a genuine desire and hunger for the Lord is enough to spark a group. One group, in turn, is enough to ignite a neighborhood, a business office, a college dormitory, or a military barracks. The resulting disciples could saturate a community with God's truth—and you could be the person to start this process.

A discussion group's goal
The kind of discussion group described in this booklet involves regular, individual Bible study preparation by each group member before the group meets together each time. Otherwise the discussions become a substitute for personal study, and the time is spent with everyone "sharing his ignorance." Those few who have prepared may not learn anything new from those who haven't, and will soon lose their motivation for being involved.

So the goal of a Bible study discussion group is to amplify the results of each person's individual Bible study through your interaction together.

A successful group—

• provides an incentive for each member to complete his personal Bible study on a regular basis.

• enables you to go beyond the limits of your own personal findings by exposing you to the ideas of others, and by stimulating further thoughts.

• creates an atmosphere of love and acceptance which stimulates honest talk about personal discoveries, questions, problems, and needs.

• builds the confidence of group members and allows them the freedom to talk about the Bible without fear of embarrassment or criticism.

• fosters positive Christian fellowship where group members can develop close personal relationships in an informal setting—you learn how to pray together and how to bear the burdens of others.

• equips growing Christians with a method for helping others grow spiritually. Small Bible study groups are one of the most effective tools to help Christians fulfill Christ's great commission to make disciples in every nation.

What discussion groups do

Group discussions are not lectures in which an infallible expert displays his knowledge to a captive audience. The lecture is unnecessary in a group discussion because the members have studied the lesson material in advance and should be able to discuss what they have learned.

Nor are group discussions conversations in which overly opinionated people carry on a dialogue. In this situation the quieter members of the group will soon lose interest and may stop coming altogether if they aren't given opportunities to share. The spontaneous interaction of a good discussion provides a setting for sharing, learning, and making new discoveries.

God's word achieves its life-changing effect on people through the ministry of the Holy Spirit. The effective group leader will act as a chairman and guide—not as an authority and teacher—because he realizes that *the Bible* is the group's authority, and *the Holy Spirit* is their teacher.

This book covers fundamental principles for leading a small Bible study discussion group. If you are planning to start a group for the first time, it will provide a thorough explanation of how to get your group started on the right foot. If you're looking for new tips to improve a study group you are already leading, reading and rereading this material will give you ideas and practical suggestions, as well as a good review of basic principles.

2. HOW TO ORGANIZE A BIBLE STUDY DISCUSSION GROUP

BACK OFF GENGHIS...
BILL'S A CHRISTIAN TOO! RIGHT, BILL?
BILL...?

Every truly successful endeavor begins with prayer. Before you invite people to a Bible study group, begin praying daily that God will attract the group members he wants, that he will unify them, and that he will enable you to lead and encourage them.

The kind of Bible study group you will have depends, of course, on the kind of people you invite to be in it. Are they couples, single adults, housewives, businessmen, senior citizens, your neighbors, your fellow church members? Are they non-Christians, new Christians, Christians with a few years of maturing, seasoned veterans, or a combination of all four?

Your Christian bookstore carries many good studies on individual topics, concerns, and books of the Bible for varying age groups and spiritual maturity levels. Be sure the study material you choose fits the needs of the group, contains lessons that are not too hard or long, and is applicable to your group member's daily lives.

If you are choosing the study material together as a group, narrow the list of possibilities to three or so, and let the group members decide by consensus which one to use. Some bookstores will allow you to take home a copy of various study materials to help you decide. (See page 4 for a partial listing of current NavPress Bible study tools.)

If you want to start a study with fellow church members, work through your pastor or other church staff, perhaps extending an invitation in your church bulletin or newsletter. Or you may want to help follow up new or immature Christians in your community or use a group setting to witness to non-Christian friends in your neighborhood or place of work. Finding the right Bible study material will help you meet their needs in the best way.

Always *personally* invite potential group members, and give them a telephone call a few days after you first invite them. Be truly concerned about them as persons, and not just as more members for your group.

Give them specific details about the study group when you're inviting people. Tell them *what* you are planning to do, *when* you plan to meet, and *how many weeks* the course of study will last. You should probably plan on the first study lasting no longer than six to eight weeks. When those few weeks are up, the group can make plans together for further study.

A neighborhood coffee hour
One way to start a Bible study discussion group in your neighborhood is to invite several people to your home one evening for coffee and dessert. Tell them about your interest in starting a group, and then ask them to join you. Tell them what the

group would be discussing so they don't come later only because of misconceptions about what they would be doing.

This coffee and dessert time shouldn't be "religious." Don't open with a prayer or use Christian jargon such as "I've been led to start a Bible study." You may be familiar with these terms but they may only scare prospective participants.

After serving refreshments and simply explaining the format of the study, suggest that they call you in the next one or two weeks *if they are interested*. Those who are *not* interested will not have to call and offer an excuse.

Don't feel hurt if everyone isn't as excited about the Bible study as you are. Not all will want to join. Just be loving, gracious, and kind to all of them so they have the freedom to make their own decisions without feeling guilty.

Try to keep the group small. You don't have to start a big program, and big groups can stifle discussion. Start with a few interested and eager people. A good group size is six, and as they become more familiar with what a Bible study group is all about they can lead other groups of their own. The natural progress of a healthy Bible study group is growth.

But don't be disappointed if you have only two or three people in the group. God is intensely interested in every individual.

Some people may accept an invitation to a Bible study group and then fail to attend. It's easy for them to forget something that is not yet part of their routine. So you may want to remind everyone of the discussion group meeting a day or so in advance. Once the group gets going this won't be necessary. By then they will have discovered for themselves the value and enjoyment of Bible study discussion.

Practical details
An uncomfortably warm or cold room, noisy children or pets, or meetings that last too long can take away from the

group's enjoyment of their time together. Here are some things that you, as the group leader, can plan in advance to lessen these distractions:

Meet in a comfortable atmosphere. The warmness of a living room, the unity of a kitchen table, or the informality of a dorm room or barracks can all lend themselves to a good teaching atmosphere. Your attitude and approach can also make the time together friendly, natural, and conducive to honest searching and sharing.

Make appropriate physical arrangements. You may want to meet in a circle so all can see and easily talk with each other. Make sure to place yourself where you see everyone clearly.

Maintain good lighting. Good lighting can not only illuminate the room, but also create a feeling of warmth.

Provide proper ventilation. Make sure the air temperature stays comfortable.

Guard against distractions. Pets, televisions, and radios take away attention from the discussion. Also, you may want to make arrangements with a babysitter to keep your children or those of other group members.

You'll discover other practical matters to take care of as you lead the group. But remember that the best preparation of all is your own *prayer*.

3. YOUR FIRST MEETING

GREAT IDEA, SUSAN — WE COULD START OFF WITH SOME WORK ON THE ATONEMENT AND THEN PERHAPS EXPLORE THE RELATIONSHIP BETWEEN THE REFORMERS' CONCEPTS OF SOTERIOLOGY AND THOSE REFLECTED BY THE ESCHATOLOGY OF THE CONTEMPORARY EVANGELICAL COMMUNITY!

It is almost impossible to overestimate the importance of your group's first meeting. The impressions created may well influence how your group progresses for weeks to come.

Remember especially during this first meeting that you will be getting together each week for a *group discussion*. You are the leader—not the director. Be unpretentious and honest. Don't put on airs of superiority, but exhibit the quiet confidence that comes from having a plan to serve the other group members, and knowing how to execute it.

Your major objective in this first meeting is to get the participants started in studying God's word together. There are three major steps to accomplishing this.

First, get acquainted with one another. You need to know one another before honest discussion and interaction can take place. As each person arrives, make sure he knows everyone else there. To help them remember each other's name, you yourself should call them by their names as often as possible.

Help them get to know one another by having each person share about himself. Remember that adults learn best in an informal, relaxed atmosphere, so as you get them to begin talking about themselves, start with what is least personal. Sharing names, hometowns, and occupations is always a good opener. If you as the leader do it first, you'll set the pace for what to cover and how long to take.

Asking unusual and unimportant questions can add some humor and help everyone stay relaxed. Instead of having all of them answer the same question, you might make cards with different questions and have everyone draw one to answer. Here are some examples:

Who was your fourth-grade teacher? Tell us something about her.

What qualities do you like best in a car design?

Who was your first girlfriend (boyfriend)? Tell us something about her.

What do you like best to do on a rainy day at home?

You can also tell what has drawn each of you to God and made you want to study the Bible. Again, you as the leader should go first in telling this.

If your group is comprised entirely of Christians, you can have each one then briefly share his testimony about coming to know Christ personally. You would not do this, of course, in an evangelistic Bible study group in which the participants are non-Christians.

Second, explain how the Bible is going to be studied and discussed in your group. Before actually beginning your explanation, pause for prayer and ask God to guide the discussion and teach all of you from his word.

It is also important that everyone adheres to an agreed-upon set of standards for the group. You, as the leader, should *suggest* these standards. Don't assume a dictatorial attitude and start telling everyone what is expected. Say something like, "Can all of us agree that we should each complete our individual preparation of the study each week before we come to our discussion meeting?" Everyone should especially agree on the importance of *completing* the individual Bible study preparation and attending the discussion meetings each week.

If you have not already done so (while recruiting the members to your group), now is the time to introduce them to the study materials, if any, which you will be using. Go over carefully the introduction and the instructions in the material. To help everyone pay close attention, go around the circle having each person read a paragraph. Stop and discuss what has been read whenever a question arises. You may want to explain in your own words more about what the later study material is about and why you think the group will enjoy it and benefit from it.

Your third step is to get them started doing the study. Enthusiasm can often be developed in this first meeting as the group members actually do a little of the study preparation. Ask them to start working individually on a small portion of the study material for the following week. (You may need to have a few Bibles to pass around for them to use.) This should probably take no more than five to ten minutes.

Then ask them to share with the group what they have discovered from this short glimpse into God's word. There may not be a great deal of time to fully discuss these observations (you can do that next week), so work at creating curiosity and anticipation for the rest of the study. You might say something like, "There isn't time to discuss it now, but I wonder if we'll discover that. . . ." Or, "I have a hunch we'll discover more about that as we complete the preparation for next week."

Especially in this first meeting, be sure not to criticize any of the responses from the group. Work at giving sincere compliments. Everyone will be encouraged by your honest praise.

As you bring to a close this time of sharing, lead the group in a brief prayer. If you have budgeted your time carefully, you shouldn't be running late.

As you adjourn, remind everyone of the time and place for your next meeting, and mention again the assigned preparation.

4. QUESTIONS— THE KEY TO GOOD DISCUSSION

A good leader helps the members of the group discover biblical truths *for themselves*. Therefore he must cultivate the ability to ask the right questions. These questions become a springboard for discussion, and will help the group members make new discoveries about what they've already studied on their own.

"You start a question," Robert Louis Stevenson said, "and it's like starting a stone. You sit quietly on the top of the hill; and away the stone goes, starting others."

Good questions are valuable because—

• They help you as the leader to evaluate the group members' understanding of the Bible.

• They cause the group members to think.

• They prevent the group leader from becoming an authority figure.

• They allow the group members to discover spiritual truth for themselves.

The Bible discussion leader asks questions to help the others become "discoverers." The leader is not a teacher. He is a guide and a participant himself. He uses questions that help the group discover, understand, and apply biblical truths.

He does this by:

launching the discussion;

guiding the discussion;

summarizing the discussion;

and helping the group members *apply* what they have learned.

A good *launching* question is one that simply asks the group members what they have discovered on their own in a particular section or question in their Bible study preparation. This means using phrases such as "What did you learn in this section about . . . ?" "What did you discover in this passage about . . . ?" "What did you observe in this question about . . . ?" "In this verse, what impressed you about . . . ?"

To *guide* the discussion means keeping it moving, and drawing out the principal thoughts the group is sharing. You can ask questions like these: "Who else would like to comment on that?" "What does someone else see in this verse?" "Does anyone else want to add something?"

When the discussion wanders away from the Bible, you may need to get the group back on track by saying, "What we're discussing is interesting, but we've left our topic. Perhaps we could discuss this more at a different time." Then you could present a thought-provoking question that draws the group back to the biblical issues you were discussing.

Often during the discussion someone will ask "What does it mean?" Discussing together an answer to this question should be valuable, because you know the group is discussing *their* concerns. But don't let the discussion go off on a tangent.

So we see that the first two important parts of your job as a discussion group leader—to *launch* and *guide* the discussion—are done almost entirely with questions.

The other two parts of your job—summarizing the discussion and helping the group members apply what they have learned—may take less of your total discussion time and depend less on questions.

To *summarize* the discussion is something you may want to do frequently throughout the group's time together each week. Your summary can be a summary of what the group has been talking about in the last few minutes, and can serve as a transition to another topic. You then simply ask another launching question about the new topic, and you're off.

In summarizing, remember to review *what the group* has discussed, rather than your own insights. Don't preach.

To carry out the fourth part of your job—helping the group members *apply what they have learned*—you can ask questions or state reminders to help them put biblical truth into practice in their lives. This could mean helping them *remember* such things as important doctrines, God's attributes, God's promises, and verses on the authority of God's word. It could also mean helping them *do* something—figuring out what steps of action you and they can take to conform your lives to God's standards. A third way of helping them make application is to discuss how each of you can use what you have learned to help someone else grow spiritually.

In asking application questions, use discretion in directing a personal question to a particular individual. Only ask an individual about his personal application when you are sure it would benefit the group present.

One way to encourage personal application of what your group is discovering in the Scriptures is to have everyone write out an intended application at the end of your discussion time. Then they can share the results of this application plan at your meeting the following week. This pattern encourages writing short-range applications and expecting God to help them apply what he has brought to their personal attention.

The importance of applying God's word to our everyday lives cannot be overly emphasized, but too often it is easily avoided. Two questions should be in the heart of every believer as he looks into the Scriptures: *Do I have the desire to know God's word?* and *Do I have the desire to do God's word?* The Bible was not given to us merely to satisfy our curiosity, but to change and redirect our lives. God gave us his word to reveal himself to us, and to evoke a response from us according to what is revealed.

How do I ask questions?

Asking questions is a powerful method for stimulating thought. So the more you plan and evaluate the questions you ask in a Bible study group, the greater will be your effectiveness as a leader.

One of the main reasons for asking questions is to help people understand biblical principles. Your questions can help them grasp the basic issue in any particular passage.

Once the group has identified this biblical principle, you can ask a follow-up question that ties in this principle to a specific situation, such as, "How could this teaching by Jesus on riches be related to how we spend our money?" This can be a real-life situation or a hypothetical one, but it should help the group realize how the principle can be practically applied, and how the Scriptures can actually change our lives.

When you ask a question, look around the group until someone answers it. Then you can ask, "What did others of you find?" or "What did someone else discover?" (these are both *guiding* questions). Again, look around the entire group, watching for anyone who wants to speak instead of pointing out a specific individual.

To begin with, the group members will probably look directly at you as they give their replies. But if you patiently persist with good guiding questions, the members will begin responding to the group instead of to the leader. Thus, true discussion will begin. Rather than being leader-centered, they will become group-centered.

The best way to learn these methods is to have your discussion questions written out beforehand.

What questions stimulate the best discussion?

The easiest rule to remember in promoting discussion is to never ask questions that can be answered simply yes or no. Questions like these rarely stimulate active thought or discussion. An example: "Do you agree with that?"

Another kind of question to avoid is a limiting question such as "What are the three great truths in this passage?" Your group members will tend to answer such a question by telling you what they think *you* think. Everyone realizes you're thinking of a specific answer—so instead of stimulating discussion, you start a mind-reading contest.

Much better are open-ended questions, each of which could have a countless variety of answers: "Why do you think this is true?" "How is this important?" "What does this truth mean for our lives today?" "Who do you think should be involved in this?" "How can we learn from this?" "Who does this apply to?"

How your questions relate to Bible study preparation

Each member of your group will have completed his study before coming to the discussion meeting. He will have followed these essential practices in his study: observation, interpretation, and application.

Observation is his effort to see exactly what the Scripture says—simply and clearly.

Interpretation is the step of determining what Scripture *means*—clarifying the meaning of a verse or passage so he can understand why the Holy Spirit included it in Scripture.

Application is his attempt to understand how to put God's word into practice—recognizing the voice of the Lord speaking personally to him, and responding accordingly in obedience.

Your *launching* questions will often focus on helping the group talk about their observations: "What did you discover in this passage about . . . ?" "What did you observe in this section on . . . ?"

Your *guiding* questions will often help the group focus on their interpretation of the Scriptures: "What did you think this meant?" "What do others of you think about that?"

Your *summary* and *application* questions and reminders will help the group members move toward practicing the Scriptures in their lives, as you review the most important things you have talked about and how they relate to each person there.

Each member of the group will have gained personal satisfaction in investigating the Scriptures on his own during the preparation time. That makes spoon-feeding them unnecessary. You won't need to lecture or teach, which could only cool their desire to learn more from the Scriptures. Instead, allow the discussion to reveal and build on what each person has already discovered on his own.

Common errors in asking questions
Try to avoid doing these things:

Asking questions that do not sound conversational. Even though you prepare and write out your questions beforehand, speak them in a conversational tone. And use your own natural vocabulary.

Being afraid of silence after asking a question. Don't be

impatient or nervous. Give everyone time to think. Waiting demonstrates your real interest and concern. Remember also to be attentive to second thoughts. Often a person will think of more to say on an issue or be able to clarify his position only after he makes his first statement. It's common to think of something else you *should* have said. If you sense someone is thinking this way, be alert enough to ask for more ideas: "Do you have more thoughts on that? Would you like to add something else?"

Limiting yourself only to asking questions. The leader is also a participant in the group. Share freely your answers and observations, but don't dominate the discussion.

Combining two questions in one. Ask one question at a time.

Asking a question that can be answered yes or no. This type of question hinders discussion—"Did Jesus die on the cross to save us?" Or, "Do you think that Jesus should be the Lord of your life?" Better questions on these subjects would be "Why do you think Jesus died on the cross?" and "In what ways do you feel Jesus should be the Lord of your life?" Starting questions with words like *can, do,* and *should* usually creates a close-ended question. Open-ended questions often begin with *why, what,* or *how.*

Asking questions that are too complex. State each question simply and clearly.

5. PREPARING A LESSON PLAN

Four ways of structuring the discussion

If your group is using question-and-answer Bible study book-lets, one of the following methods is probably most appro-priate for leading the group into meaningful discussion of what they have prepared individually.

Method 1: Go around the group in order with the first person giving his answer to question one, the next person answering question two, and so on. Other group members are free to make additional comments after an answer has been given.

This is a good way to get young Christians started in Bible study discussion. It gives them a sense of security and confidence. They can see where the discussion is and where it is going. As the leader, you won't need to rely much in this method on discussion questions you've prepared beforehand.

Method 2: The questions are still answered in order, but anyone in the group is free to be the first to answer. The leader can read a question from the Bible study booklet and say, "Who would like to answer this question?" Or he might not read the question but ask instead, "Who would take question five for us?"

A danger of this approach is that some may dominate the discussion while others sit back quietly. Sometimes the leader may need to ask a quieter person, "John, would you be willing to answer question six for us?"

Method 3: In the third method, you also go from question to question as you did in methods 1 and 2, but you rely greatly on additional discussion questions which you prepared beforehand for drawing out a deeper response to each question in the Bible study material.

Method 4: Here you rely completely on an outline and discussion questions which you have prepared before the group's meeting. Rather than discussing each question in the Bible study booklet, you go section by section. You could launch the discussion on a group of questions about prayer, for example, by saying, "From what you studied in this first section of the chapter, what do you believe are the main benefits of prayer?"

One or more of the group members can respond by telling what impressed them most in these questions on prayer, and you can keep the discussion going by asking some of the guiding questions you have prepared.

In this method the emphasis is definitely on the group. The discussion should be open and spontaneous, within the boundaries of the lesson content.

It is important, however, that the members of the group come to this kind of discussion meeting with their lessons prepared, since this individual preparation serves as the basis for meaningful discussion.

What is a lesson plan?
A lesson plan is a written statement of what you want to accomplish and how you intend to accomplish it during your group's time together. A lesson plan will help you organize the way you would like your group's discussion to develop. A well prepared lesson plan is to the discussion group leader what an up-to-date map is to the traveler.

Having a written lesson plan in hand as you lead the discussion time will help you progress confidently through the group's time together. It will also help you to keep the group on the most important topics. Thus, you can use your time wisely.

Follow the steps in preparing a lesson plan:

1. *Write an outline based on the study material each group member is preparing beforehand.* If the study material is a chapter from a Bible study booklet, the subheadings throughout the chapter should provide a good basis for your outline.

The outline is the basic framework which underlies a particular passage or topical study. It consists of a few subpoints that logically break down the study material into smaller sections. Like a builder looking at the blueprint for a building, you can look at an outline to see the basic framework of your study material.

In leading a discussion group, an outline will help you:
• provide a general direction for the study;
• prepare discussion questions;
• evaluate the progress of the discussion;
• and stress the content of the study material.

2. *Write down your objective for the lesson.* If the chapter you are discussing in your Bible study booklet is on "Knowing God's Will," your objective could be, "To learn how to practically seek and know God's will."

A good discussion group leader begins with an objective

clearly in mind. Don't fall into the trap of "flying by the seat of your pants."

An objective is a brief statement that summarizes what the group should understand and apply by the end of the discussion period. It should be stated clearly in one or two short sentences.

A clear objective will help you do three things:

• It will tell you where you are heading with the discussion and give you direction for your questions.

• It will help you evaluate progress at any point during the discussion. With this evaluation, you can make adjustments when necessary.

• It will allow you to make decisions along the way as to what to discuss. If a tangent issue arises, you can direct the group back to the main goal and temporarily table the tangent.

Often the chapter titles themselves in a Bible study booklet will be explicit enough to help you determine the discussion objective.

3. *Prepare one or two launching questions, several guiding questions, and one or two application questions for each section of your outline.*

4. *Plan an introduction that orients the group to the subject.* One possible way of doing this is to go over together the introductory matter that is in the Bible study booklet itself. Most question-and-answer Bible studies have a paragraph or two which introduce the subject of each chapter in an interesting way. Reading this passage aloud will draw everyone into the topic.

Once the subject has been introduced, plan to stop and pray. The prayer will vary, but the purpose is to thank God for the time together and to ask him to teach all of you through the discussion. Ask God for guidance. Because you have already prepared the lesson and read the introductory paragraphs, you can ask him to teach you specifically about the subject you will be discussing tonight.

Remember that the Scriptures are the source of truth. Plan to ask someone in the group to look up and read aloud some of the verses listed for the study questions as you discuss your answers.

Remember too that your own attitude is a key factor in the group's enthusiasm. Decide beforehand to develop a genuine interest in each person's remarks, and expect to learn from them. Concentrate on developing acceptance and concern in the group. Avoid a businesslike atmosphere.

5. *Plan how you will conclude the study.* This conclusion should include a brief review of what your group has discussed, and a clear statement about the assignment for the next meeting. It is usually best also to pray together before breaking up.

Close in prayer as a group. Thank God for the time and the truths revealed during the study and discussion. Be specific. Ask him for wisdom and understanding in applying what has been discovered.

In giving the next week's assignment, plan to state the topic or title of the next chapter. Along with the assignment, create an air of expectancy by asking a motivating question such as, "If this God who loves us were to reveal himself to us, what would he be like?" or, "Why was it important for Christ to come in the form of a man?" This technique causes the group to have a questioning attitude while completing the assignment, and creates a natural introduction for the next week's discussion time.

Remember to budget your time so that you don't keep the group too late. Two to five minutes should be enough for the introduction, and about the same amount of time should be reserved for the conclusion. The rest of your time should be divided according to the different sections in your outline.

To ensure that the discussion adequately covers everything you feel is important, maintain the time limits you have set for each section. Sometimes the discussion of a particularly interesting point lasts longer than you intended. Then you will need to shorten or perhaps even omit the next section.

Your total meeting time should probably not exceed ninety minutes, and one hour might be best. If your time is running out and you need to skip a question or two, it's usually best to skip guiding questions. Always try to include application questions and discussion for each section. Your goal in Bible study is not, of course, to have something to discuss, but to change your lives.

Your lesson plan will serve as a guide for the discussion. Don't worry, however, if you're unable to follow it exactly. Use it simply as a guide. Be sure to review your lesson plan, especially the objective and your outline, before the group gets together.

Your lesson plan isn't intended to restrict you as a discussion leader but to give you a plan which you can always refer to. With this plan in mind, you'll have the freedom to let the discussion move spontaneously in new directions, knowing how and when to move it back to the main subjects of your outline.

When you review your discussion time, you will notice many things have taken place. Group tension and conflict may have arisen from the personal interaction of members. Some were very talkative, others very quiet. This is normal in the life of a discussion group. In fact, group tensions are often indications of a living and maturing group! Maintaining control in these situations is one of your functions as a leader.

As you prepare for and lead discussion groups over a period of time, you'll become more confident in your developing style of leadership. You will learn how to plan and ask questions and guide the discussion more effectively, and how to respond appropriately to group members in various situations.

Leading a Bible discussion group is a privilege given to you by God. Be sure to thank him for the opportunity to guide people as they discover the truths of God's word. Trust him to help you become increasingly effective as a discussion leader.

6. PREPARING GOOD QUESTIONS

O.K. GUYS—
HOW CAN WE APPLY
THIS TRUTH TO OUR LIVES?

There is an art to asking questions. Anyone who *wants to* can learn the skill of asking good questions.

Here are three criteria for good questions:

Good questions are *clear*.

Good questions are *relevant*.

Good questions *stimulate discussion*.

These criteria will help you formulate and evaluate your questions. Once you've prepared some questions, think about how people in your study would respond to them. Then revise your questions if necessary.

The *launching* questions you prepare should be carefully selected because they initiate meaningful discussion on a topic. They will determine to a large extent both what you will discuss and the response you will receive. Since you are trying to stimulate discussion, ask general questions that have several possible answers. For example, don't say, "What did God create?" This limits the response of the group. If you ask, "What did you learn about creation from your study this week?" the responses will include a variety of personal observations.

These launching questions should be simple and short. Avoid using *and* or *but*. These words usually introduce a second question.

Also, be sure your launching questions relate to the study preparation done during the previous week.

Your *guiding* questions will help open up, deepen, illustrate, or clarify the discussion started by the launching questions. These questions encourage the group members to go beyond their initial observations.

One of your goals is to help the group understand more fully the *meaning* of the truths discovered. Ask yourself what words or phrases or ideas in the study passages may not be clearly understood, and think of questions that will help clarify their meaning.

Application questions are hard to formulate, but they can be the link between Bible study and daily living. Each group member needs to really live with the passages you are studying, and to ask God to reveal how it should be applied in everyday living.

Here are examples of application questions:

What can you do in the coming week to better glorify God as part of his creation?

What assurance do you have that you are part of God's family?

What difference should your assurance of salvation make in your life today?

How can you follow Jesus Christ's example of servanthood in the way you respond to and help other members of your family this week?

Clarity
To evaluate your prepared written questions for clarity, use these standards:

> Can the question be understood?
> Can it be easily remembered?
> Does it generally avoid the words *and* and *but*?
> Does it avoid raising unnecessary problems?

Relevance
Use these standards to evaluate the relevance of your prepared questions:

> What is the underlying purpose of the question?
> What answer does it expect or suggest?
> To whom is it directed?
> Does it relate to truth already known?
> Does the group have enough information to answer it?
> Does it focus attention on the main point?
> Does it call for a possible and practical response?
> Will it lead to a clear understanding of the passage?

Stimulating discussion
Use these standards to help you evaluate how well your written questions can promote discussion:

> Does the question get the group's attention?
> Does it lead to personal involvement?
> Does it leave room for individual creative expression?
> Does it give everyone an opportunity to respond?
> Is it aimed at the group's personal understanding?
> Does it avoid embarrassing any of the group members?

Involvement and urgency
Notice in Mark 8:27-29 how Jesus helped his disciples to think first objectively (without being personally involved) and only then subjectively (being personally involved) about the im-

portant matter of who he was. In verse 27 he asked them, "Who do *people* say I am?" Then, after they answered, he asked them, "Who do *you* say I am?"

In the following list of questions, notice the increasing degree of involvement from one to the next:

"What should people do about this?"

"What should people in our church do about this?"

"What should we do about this?"

"What *will* we do about this?"

The last question reflects not only personal involvement, but urgency. To make it even more urgent, you could ask, "What will we do about this *now*?"

Examples of prepared questions

Here is a list of sample questions you may want to look over to further stimulate your thinking as you plan your questions for your next Bible study group meeting. Most of these are guiding and launching questions written for various chapters in the *Design for Discipleship* Bible study series from NavPress.

What one aspect of Jesus' life impresses you most?

Why can't God ignore our sin?

What impressed you most from this prayer of Jesus?

Why do we need the Holy Spirit in our lives?

How important is love in our relationship with God?

How do you know the Bible is God's word?

What do you think it means to let the word of Christ
    dwell richly in us?

What does it mean to pray in Jesus' name?

How do we grow in grace?

What is involved in surrendering to Christ's lordship?

When do you keep cares and worries to yourself, instead
    of casting them on the Lord?

What promises from God are you claiming for your life?

How does the Holy Spirit guide us?

How would you explain this passage to someone else?
What effect does impurity have on your relationship with God?
What are some of the kinds of suffering we may have to endure?
Who does God say he is?
Which of God's attributes do you feel you know the most about?
What can we learn from Jesus' encounter with Satan?

Choose three or four of these sample questions, and imagine what kind of discussion they would lead to in your Bible study group.

Never tell when you can ask
Remember that as the leader you do not have to be a walking biblical encyclopedia with all the answers. Leading means guiding the group in such a way that each person, including yourself, amplifies and clarifies the personal insights gained through individual study. Giving the group time to talk and get acquainted will help create an environment where each member can freely share his discoveries, questions, comments, and feelings.

Your job as a discussion group leader is to help them discover truth for themselves. Don't tell them something they could conclude for themselves if you were to ask them the right questions. Never tell when you can ask. Have good questions prepared that will allow the group to draw their own conclusions.

7. MORE ABOUT QUESTIONS

SO HOW SHOULD WE REACT TO THIS RESPONSE AND WHAT DOES IT MEAN TO US AS BELIEVERS, DO YOU FEEL?

Christian educator H. H. Horne wrote in *Jesus: The Master Teacher* (1920) that Jesus "came not to answer questions, but to ask them; not to settle men's souls, but to provoke them." Questions made up the heart of Jesus Christ's teaching method.

From his example we can learn that our job as discussion group leaders is to help others discover truth for themselves. The following guidelines will help you accomplish this.

Use questions that deal with feelings as well as facts
Facts will tell you what a person knows. His feelings will tell you how he really feels, and convictions are formed internally as people learn to express verbally how they feel about certain issues.

Ask questions such as, "How do you respond inwardly

to these claims Jesus makes?" "How do you feel about these teachings on love?" "What do you think about that?" "How do you react to that?"

Deal with people's true interests

Questions that come closest to people's true interests will get the best answers. Learn how to identify a person's frame of reference. Find out not only *what* he wants to talk about, but *how* he wants to talk about it. Take something from his answer to formulate your next question to the group. Use his own words. People appreciate hearing their own thoughts being used.

Answer questions with questions

Often people may ask the leader a question when their real desire is to tell you what they think. "Don't you think that . . . ?" and "Do you think that . . . ?" are examples of this. A good way to avoid a premature answer is to respond by saying, "What do you think?" This is what they really want—an opportunity to express their views.

Sometimes people will try to force you to defend yourself. Their purpose is to show you that they disagree with you. By responding with "What do you think?" you can allow them to fully express themselves without your having to take a controversial position.

Learn how to use direct questions

A direct question—"Bill, is Christ the Lord of your life?"—asks a person to take an open stand and declare a position. Be careful not to use such questions too soon in your relationships with the group members, or they may become offended. Be sure you have their confidence first. Use impersonal and indirect questions first—"How can you tell that Jesus is Lord of someone's life?"

Avoid questions that assume an answer

Don't oversuggest answers in your questions. Lead and direct your group toward answers, but don't drag the group into them. Rhetorical questions with obvious answers fall into this category: "The purpose of evangelism is to reach the unsaved, isn't it?" Better would be, "What do you think the purpose of evangelism is?"

Use questions that focus on a specific item

Use words and phrases in your questions that cause one's mind to focus on only one key idea. "What was the most interesting thing you learned from this passage?" is better than "What did you learn from this passage?"

Keep the discussion going

Short guiding questions such as "What else did you notice?" or "What do you mean by that?" can keep the discussion moving by drawing additional responses from the group. Other examples: "What else can you add to that?" "Could you explain that more fully?" "Could you rephrase that statement?" "Would you explain that?" "What reason can you give for that?" Sometimes these questions can redirect the group's attention to a different individual: "Mary, what do you think about that?"

8. ROLES PEOPLE PLAY

In the following lists, Professor Howard Hendricks of Dallas Theological Seminary describes some of the roles people play in a group situation. You may find these helpful in evaluating your group. You could read the lists aloud to your group, and then discuss their responses to them. This evaluation can help all of you see yourselves in a new light.

Immature roles

The onlooker | Content to be a silent spectator. Only nods, smiles, and frowns. Other than this, he is a passenger instead of a crew member.

The monopolizer | Brother Chatty. Rambles roughshod over the rest of the conversation with his verbal dexterity. Tenaciously clings to his right to say what he thinks—even without thinking.

The belittler   This is Mr. Gloom. He minimizes the con-
                tributions of others. Usually has three
                good reasons why some opinion is wrong.
The wisecrack   Feels called to a ministry of humor. Mister
                Cheerio spends his time as the group
                playboy. Indifferent to the subject at hand,
                he is always ready with a clever remark.
The hitchhiker Never had an orginal thought in his life.
                Unwilling to commit himself. Sits on the
                sidelines until others reach a conclusion,
                then jumps on the bandwagon.
The pleader   Chronically afflicted with obsessions.
                Always pleading for some cause or action.
                Feels led to share this burden frequently.
                One-track mind.
The sulker   Lives with a resentful mood. The group
                won't always agree entirely with his view,
                so he sulks.

Mature roles

The proposer   Initiates ideas and action. Keeps things
                moving.
The encourager Brings others into the discussion. En-
                courages others to contribute. Emphasizes
                the value of their suggestions and com-
                ments. Stimulates others to greater activity
                by approval and recognition.
The clarifier   Has the ability to step in when confusion,
                chaos, and conflict occur. He defines the
                problem concisely. Points out the issues
                clearly.
The analyzer   Examines the issues closely. Weighs sug-
                gestions carefully. Never accepts anything
                without first thinking it through.

The explorer	Always moving into new and different areas. Probing relentlessly. Never satisfied with the obvious or the traditional viewpoints.
The mediator	Promotes harmony between members—especially those who have trouble agreeing. Seeks to find conclusions acceptable to all.
The synthesizer	Able to put the pieces together from different ideas and viewpoints.

9. CONSTRUCTIVE GROUP TENSION

In most discussion groups, controversy and tension are avoided like the plague. Many associate conflict with dissension and strife, so they try to steer any trace of disagreement down a deserted alley or off a steep cliff.

Some disagreements, it is true, are caused by misguided opinions, petty issues, and false doctrines. But not all disagreements are bad, wrong, or un-Christian. The group that sails along with its members always giving the "right" answers may be the group that isn't thinking about truly important issues.

Discussing a controversial issue may be well worth the time it takes. Profitable discussions can take place after a question causes tense disagreement. When this happens, the group leader can point the members to God's word as the final authority, instead of traditional or "logical" thinking.

Three stages
Healthy group tension is best when it occurs in three stages: *personalization, confrontation,* and *clarification.*

1.   Before you deliberately introduce a controversial subject, it's best to develop a relaxed atmosphere—the *personalization* stage. This should have been accomplished once your group has been meeting for some time, and all the members have become well acquainted with each other and accepting of each other.

2.   The *confrontation* stage begins when you introduce the possibility of tension. You do this by asking questions that lead the group members down the "streets of the unknown response" to the eventual goal of agreement based on the Scriptures.

You can create a difference of opinion in a variety of ways. Having each member respond in turn to a controversial question, staging a debate, or intentionally taking the opposite view on an issue can create the kind of unsettledness that forces the group into the Bible to find true answers.

Here are examples of the kind of questions that can generate confrontation:

• Questions that require a decision—"Which is better, to do what is right when you don't feel like it, or to wait to act until you have the right motive and desires?"

• Questions that imply something that isn't true—"Why do we need to avoid contact with non-Christians as much as possible?"

• Questions about difficult or questionable topics— "Why does God allow suffering? Is there a biblical basis for the women's liberation movement? Should a Christian go to war?"

3.   In the *clarification* stage, the leader takes control and directs the group toward biblical conclusions. His goal is to get the group into the Scriptures to find truths and principles that

address the controversial issue. (Sometimes resolution occurs when the group realizes that the Bible *does not* give a specific answer, but allows room for several opinions.)

Be ready with summary questions and a summary statement to put into focus the biblical conclusions the group has found. From there you can apply the conclusions in various ways to your lives.

Be cautious

You must, of course, be careful with confrontation questions that cause tension. Animosity, division, and strife can sometimes be caused by group tension, as the apostle Paul warned: "Don't have anything to do with foolish and stupid arguments, because you know they produce quarrels" (2 Timothy 2:23). Keep this verse in mind as your group considers controversial issues.

Aim toward love and unity—"Be completely humble and gentle; be patient, bearing with one another in love. Make every effort to keep the unity of the Spirit through the bond of peace" (Ephesians 4:2-3). But don't feel you must avoid group tension at all costs, for it can lead to a more diligent search for biblical truth.

10. TURNING OBSTACLES INTO OPPORTUNITIES

Any discussion group will have its problems. But they can be turned into opportunities with proper understanding and handling.

How to control talkative members

When one or two group members seem to be monopolizing the discussion, calling for contributions from others often helps: "What do the rest of you think?" or "Jack, what ideas do you have about this?"

In some situations you may have to take control of the discussion more strongly, and you may have to talk privately with the "talker," explaining the necessity of group participation. You may be able to enlist him to help you draw others in. This will help him become more sensitive to the contributions of other people.

How to get back on track

A verbal recognition of the fact that the discussion has gotten too far off on a tangent can usually help you get back to more relevant topics. You could say, "This is interesting. However, we've left our topic. Perhaps we could discuss this further after we talk more about. . . ." Or you may present a thought-provoking question to draw the discussion back to the initial topic. At times, you can suggest tabling the tangent until after the discussion, when those who want to can talk about it further. Having an accepting attitude toward the tangent is important. Maintain respect for each member's opinions.

How to handle "wrong" answers

Never tell a group member he is wrong. If someone says something that you are quite sure is inaccurate or unbiblical, you may want to solicit a viewpoint from someone else: "Okay, what do others think?" or "Does anyone know other Scripture passages that may help us here?" You may want to restate the issue, or ask another question that would help clarify or stimulate further thought. Always keep others from losing "face" or becoming embarrassed because of a wrong answer.

How to handle silence

Don't be afraid of pauses, or try to fill in silent moments. If you give everyone time to think, *they* will bring up good points and ask good questions as the discussion progresses. By being patient, you may be surprised with the number of excellent thoughts the group comes up with. These silent times may seem uncomfortable, but don't be embarrassed or feel as if you must say something.

How to handle difficult questions

Don't be afraid of saying "I don't know" when a difficult question is asked. If you don't know the answer, don't pretend to.

You can always look for the answer later, or ask someone else in the group to research it. There is no merit in being thought of as a "know-it-all."

Getting through all the study material
Make a determined effort to cover in your discussion as much as possible of the assigned study material. Continually getting bogged down in minor details and tangents can have a demoralizing effect on the group. Moving ahead, however, gives a feeling of accomplishment and success. If you have trouble getting through everything you want to in a discussion meeting, you may need to cut back on the amount of assigned preparation each week.

How to liven up a dull group
Your group will respond to your own attitude. Pray for your own sincere enthusiasm. If you want them to be enthusiastic, you must be that way too. The right source for this excitement is a desire to know God himself, a desire for his word, and a sincere commitment to be a disciple of Jesus Christ. You, as the leader, must demonstrate these convictions. Don't expect them from others if you don't have them yourself.

If your group seems to be lethargic, ask yourself whether you are demonstrating a true devotion for God and his word, and a strong belief in the relevance of God's word to our lives today. Think through these issues carefully. What can you do to give more glory to God in the way you lead this group?

How to help your group apply the Scriptures to their lives
Expect God to speak through his word to each person in the group. The Holy Spirit will bring the Scriptures to bear upon their consciences and their lives. Try to help the group see the specific relevance of God's word for their everyday lives. Learn to ask effective application questions, beginning with

"What does this mean to you?" and "Is there anything we can do about this in our lives today?" Learn how to share your own application plans with honesty and humility. Openness on your part will help them feel more open.

Learn to show positive reinforcement
Acknowledge individual responses frequently with positive comments such as "That's good," or "That's a very thoughtful answer." It's best not to overdo positive comments, but most discussion leaders probably err on the side of not saying them enough.

Help increase listening ability
Some members of your group may tend to think more about what they want to say rather than about what others are saying. They become preoccupied with their own thoughts. One way to help them get rid of this lapse in listening is to occasionally have a group member summarize what has just been said by the previous person. Before doing this, you may want to announce to the group that you would like to do it as an exercise in helping the group become better listeners.

11. AIDS TO CREATIVITY

Using a variety of approaches in leading your group can add zest to your discussions. What can you do to learn scriptural truth more creatively?

Many familiar objects become teaching tools when used properly. A drop of dye in a jar of water can be used to illustrate the spread of the gospel throughout the world. A model or picture of the human body might stimulate discussion on the role of the church as Christ's body. A horse's bridle can help illustrate the principle from James 3 about the importance of our speech.

Newspaper cartoons often illustrate a biblical principle and add a bit of humor at the same time. Articles clipped from newspapers or magazines can also illustrate truth.

A map of Bible lands will help the group visualize action in various passages from throughout the Bible. You can also use charts, posters, puppets, models, photographs, or photographic slides. Taped messages by Christian pastors and teachers can add variety and lead to good discussion.

Other ideas to consider:

> games organized around biblical principles
>
> field trips—to churches, various mission offices, biblical conferences, and so on
>
> ministry trips for service to the poor or evangelism
>
> dramatizations—portray biblical characters, or modern-day people struggling to apply biblical truth in today's culture
>
> helpful charts, graphs, and diagrams
>
> debates
>
> brainstorming session on certain ideas or principles

Sources for ideas include your church library, community library, and Christian bookstore. You can also write to publishers for listings of visual aids. Ask for catalogues and listings of films, slides, overhead transparencies, and so on.

When developing visual aids and teaching tools, be sure to keep them simple and clear. They should include only the essentials, and they need to be relevant to your group's interests and needs.

Ask various group members occasionally to come up with teaching tools and visual aids. They'll enjoy the opportunity to play a special part in a group meeting.

Visual aids and teaching tools can accentuate and strengthen learning in these ways:

• They catch the group's interest. They get attention, and bring needs and curiosity to the surface.

• They stimulate talking, listening, and learning.

• They clarify words and concepts in easy-to-remember ways.

Be alert to any opportunity to make Bible study and discussion more fun and more imaginative.

12. INTRODUCING CONVERSATIONAL PRAYER

...AND ALSO LORD PLEASE BLESS ALL THE NICE MISSIONARIES IN KENYA, UGANDA, ETHIOPIA, LITHUANIA, GUATEMALA, BRAZIL, INDONESIA, TAIWAN, KOREA, BORA BORA...

Does praying together in a group make you nervous? If your answer is yes, you're not alone. Many of the people in your group probably feel the same way.

Most Christians seldom pray aloud in a church group. They may be afraid of sounding stupid, of not knowing what to pray, or—worst of all—of making "mistakes."

Their fears can be allayed with some positive experiences in group prayer. Your job, as the leader, is to let them see how praying as a group can be a unique time of worship—not something to dread at the end of a study.

Actually, praying together is vital for an effective discussion group. After the members have discussed their biblical discoveries and applications, a time of praise, petition, and thanksgiving will be the next most natural step.

In this time of prayer, you can remind the group that they

are a team learning to pray together. To do this, they should forget ritualism and religious sounding phrases, and concentrate instead on saying things they really mean, and saying them in their own words. Praying exactly what you think or feel requires honesty and openness with the Lord.

The person praying doesn't have to be concerned with the form of the prayer, or with how well he sounds to other group members. All he has to do is communicate with God from his heart.

Remind the group that they aren't being pressured to pray aloud with the group. Allow them to work on this at their own speed. Most of them probably want to pray aloud, but they need to feel the encouragement of the group to do so. God will bring all this about in his own time.

Here are several guidelines for conversational prayer:

As the leader, pray first. Unless you are led otherwise, pray first and use the words *I, me,* and *my* instead of *we, us,* and *our.* Speak for yourself, rather than for everyone.

After you pray, someone else may be led by the Holy Spirit to pray on the same subject. He is simply continuing your prayer with hardly a break in thought.

Don't spend too much time sharing prayer requests before actually praying. Much of your valuable prayer time can be spent in mentioning prayer requests to each other rather than praying. Usually the person with a burden to pray for someone or something will be the first to initiate prayer about it as you bow together.

Pray about one topic at a time. Pray topically as much as possible. One person may pray about a sick friend, and the next person can stay on that topic by asking for strength for the sick person's family. Then another could pray that the family's financial and emotional needs will be met. After everyone who wants to pray on this topic has done so, the group can go on to another topic.

Listen. Each of you will want to pray in your heart along with the person who is verbally praying. This will make your prayer time more meaningful.

Pray briefly. When each person prays about only one aspect of the topic, he can pray again sooner about something else after others have prayed about the topic. This helps everyone stay alert and involved in what is being prayed.

Pray spontaneously, rather than in sequence. Don't pray around the circle, but let each person pray whenever he desires to pray. If six subjects are prayed about in the conversational prayer time, you or anyone else in the group may want to pray about only three of them. None of you should feel obligated to pray for something about which you are uninformed.

Praying spontaneously doesn't mean praying thoughtlessly. Be sensitive to the Holy Spirit's careful leading about what you would like to pray.

Also, *pray audibly* so everyone can hear you.

What to pray for
As you start praying as a group, often there will be a few moments of silence while the members quiet their hearts and focus their attention on communicating with God.

Normally the first focus of your prayer together should be *praising and thanking God.* Someone may start praising him for his power, and another for his love and faithfulness. One may thank him for a neighbor who recently trusted Christ, and another may thank him for new discoveries being made in his individual Bible study.

Then you may pray for *needs within the group.* The members will find their relationships with each other will grow more personal as they pray for each other. They will also acquire an increased desire to pray for each other during the week.

Next you might pray for *needs outside the group*. Obviously, the number of needs is limitless, but it's more important to do a thorough job of praying for a few items than to scatter the prayers over too wide a range.

By praying conversationally you'll experience a new excitement about praying in a group. You will also find that it leads to more praying—both in the group and when you are alone—and to a greater awareness of God at work in your life.

Jesus said, "If two of you on earth agree about anything you ask for, it will be done for you by my Father in heaven. For where two or three come together in my name, there am I with them" (Matthew 18:19-20).

13. EVALUATING THE DISCUSSION

Here are questions that may help you as you evaluate each of your group's discussions:

1. Was I familiar enough with the material to feel free in leading the discussion?

2. Did everyone take part in the discussion? Or was it a lecture (with me doing most of the talking) or a conversation among only two or three of us?

3. Did we keep to the subject without wandering?

4. Did I frequently summarize the main ideas that were brought up by the group?

5. Did the discussion lead to further understanding of the truths the group members discovered in their personal Bible study?

6. Did we discuss adequately how we can apply what we learned to our lives?

7. Did I listen well to everyone who spoke?

8. Was I sensitive to the individual needs of the group members?

9. Were there any tangents in the discussion that I didn't handle well?

10. Did I follow my lesson plan closely?

11. Was each person in the group stimulated to contribute his best thoughts to the discussion?

12. Did the group members listen well to each other?

13. Did the meeting end on time?

These questions can stimulate further thinking as to what is expected of you as a group leader. Continue to ask the Lord for wisdom in fulfilling your responsibility to this group of people.

Three traps in evaluation

As you evaluate your skill as a discussion group leader, be aware of the following traps.

Comparing yourself with others. Comparison is a denial of God's special place for you. Each individual is unique and the Lord has given all of us special abilities that need to be developed.

Discouragement. When the discussion doesn't meet your expectations, you may become discouraged by focusing on what went wrong. But be sure your recognition of obstacles and mistakes stimulates you to make improvements. Don't allow Satan to discourage you. God is honored when his word goes forth, and he is the God of encouragement.

Giving up. Don't throw in the towel. God will reward your faithfulness. Start where you are and move in the direction of progress. In due time, you will prosper.

Remember not to focus your evaluation only on the negative—the mistakes and problems. What went right? What was good in this discussion?

Make an effort to maintain these strong points in future weeks, as God's word is studied, discussed, and applied more and more effectively.

The group member's perspective

As your group's effectiveness grows, each group member should be able to say these five things as he evaluates your discussion time:

• I feel that we went right into the Scriptures rather than only touching lightly on them.

• I feel we interacted primarily with the Scriptures rather than with the personal opinions of the leader or of others in the group.

• I feel I have a better understanding of the Scriptures than I had before I came to this discussion meeting.

• I feel our time together wasn't wasted on generalities or meaningless religious traditions.

• I feel I have been challenged, comforted, encouraged, and instructed practically by the Holy Spirit.

At some time you may want to have the group members answer the following questions, either individually on a written questionnaire, or together as a group following one of your discussion times.

1. What was the most exciting thing you learned this week from our discussion time?

2. What is one way you would like to improve our discussion group?

3. What would you say is the purpose of our group?

4. Is this discussion group giving you help in applying the Scriptures to your life?

5. Is this group helping you to better understand yourself as a person? If so, how?

6. Do you feel like an important part of this group? Why or why not?

7. Is this group and our discussion time together helping you to meet personal needs in your life? If so, how?

8. Do you feel that other members of this group truly care about how you are doing spiritually?

9. Are you becoming better disciplined and more committed in truly following Christ each day? If so, how?

10. Especially in prayer, Bible reading and study, witnessing, and fellowship, are you doing what you should to maintain a close walk with Christ?

Three ways you might discourage your group
Here are three ways in which a leader can easily discourage a Bible study discussion group:

Rushing the lesson. Because you may have a lot you want to cover in the group's discussion, you may become frustrated because of the short amount of time you have together. If you transfer this tension to the way you lead the group, they too can become frustrated. They may feel you are trying to go over too much too fast.

Examining the Scriptures too lightly. Sometimes you may be tempted to skip here and there around the Bible, briefly touching on several cross-references to make a point without thoroughly examining the particular passage at hand. Give everyone time to think about and absorb the Scriptures you look at.

Monopolizing the discussion. It's easy to begin a spontaneous sermon to share your brilliant observations and ideas, instead of getting into the Scriptures together and helping each other discover truth. Remember that people are hungry to know what the Bible says—not what you say. Keep your finger close to your own "off" button.

Keep these three possible mistakes in mind if your group seems to be discouraged.

14. IMPROVING YOUR LEADERSHIP

Here are more guidelines for improving your effectiveness as a Bible study discussion group leader:

Know the Bible study material well

Take extra time to dig a little deeper as you look at the passages your group will be discussing. There's no substitute for your own diligent and prayerful preparation. Don't get sidetracked from the priority of intensive personal study each week.

Be excited about the discoveries made by the group

Don't reserve your excitement only for what you yourself are discovering in the Scriptures. Get excited about what others are learning and show it—even if it is something that you learned long ago.

Utilize your sense of humor

Well-timed humor—appropriate to your group and to the context of what you are studying—can promote spontaneity and freedom, giving a more favorable environment for discussion. Develop your own style of humor, rather than trying to imitate others.

Be enthusiastic

Even as the leader, you may not come up with the best observations, interpretations, and applications of the Scriptures. But you should be the one with the most enthusiasm. Help make each discussion meeting unforgettable. Ask God to give you a spirit of enthusiasm both as you prepare the lesson and as you lead it.

Learn how to uncover and meet needs

Identify with the weaknesses of your group members, and help them see how the Scriptures can meet their needs.

One of the biggest ministries you can have as a discussion group leader is to pray regularly for all the members of the group. The Lord will honor this heartfelt conviction and concern.

Remember too that giving personal, individual attention to the group members outside the group's time together can be a good opportunity for fellowship and meeting needs.

15. TRAINING OTHERS TO LEAD

As each member of your group experiences personal spiritual growth, one or more of them may soon have the ability and desire to become a discussion group leader himself. Be sensitive to this, and consider whether you would like to train someone in the group as your assistant. This person could eventually replace you or be the leader of another group.

When choosing an assistant, look for someone who will—

• pray with you for the other group members on a regular basis.

• help you lead the group more effectively by reviewing the evaluation with you after each session. You can discuss with him what happened and why, and how to improve. He may often be able to see what is happening more clearly than you because he is not under the pressure of constantly asking questions.

• learn how to lead a group himself, so that if you must be absent he can take over for you.

• be prepared to begin and lead another group. If your group grows too large and you need to divide, your assistant will be the logical person to lead the new group.

If your group does divide, remind them that growing too large by not dividing would hinder the advantages of small group discussion—intimate fellowship, personal involvement with everyone, plenty of opportunities for everyone to talk, the ease with which the entire group can meet in anyone's living room, and so on.

Help the new leader arrange a place for the new group to meet. Let all the members know about the new arrangements. Allow the new leader to exercise his responsibilities, but also be available for giving advice and encouragement.

The process of multiplication and growth will continue as your former assistant finds someone in his new group to become *his* assistant, to be trained for starting yet another group.

16. HOW TO LEAD BIBLE STUDY GROUPS FOR NON-CHRISTIANS

Your non-Christian friends and neighbors will often be interested in "investigative" Bible study groups in which they can examine closely the claims of Jesus Christ. It is important in such a group for you as the leader to communicate to them that all of you are learning together. Don't try to be a lecturer.

Have a casual manner and a warm and friendly attitude. Develop a relaxed and open atmosphere in which each person feels he can say anything he honestly feels, and that his friendship with you is not contingent upon his reactions in the group. Convey total acceptance for each person.

As the leader, take charge in an inoffensive way. The group looks to you for leadership, and you must provide it.

You may want to have the group members commit themselves to be a part of the group for a certain period of time—perhaps four weeks or so.

The five steps explained below are important ones in the process of planning and leading an investigative Bible study group for non-Christians.

Association
You must have friendly contact with non-Christians to truly influence them. Consider the following guidelines.

1. Find people whom you have common interests with, and are comfortable with.

2. When they discover you are "religious," they may try to get you to talk about it. You might want to discuss with them only a few spiritual things that will motivate them for further and more detailed discussion.

3. Don't try to reform them. You are not responsible for changing their habits and lifestyle. They must understand the gospel first, and experience a personal encounter with Jesus Christ.

4. Don't pounce on those who you think may be willing to come to the study group, but first take a genuine interest in their lives. Listen to them. Later you may want to discuss their thoughts and problems, and mention some statements from Scripture that relate to your conversation.

Invitation
Actually inviting these people to be a part of an investigative Bible study group will take courage. The following suggestions may be of help.

1. Keep the group small (six to eight people).

2. Pray for several days about making the invitations before you actually invite them.

3. If you are inviting a couple, it is best to make the invitation when both husband and wife are present.

4. Offer the invitation at a relaxed social time together.

5. Let them know how many times the group would be

meeting, how long each meeting would last, what you would do at each meeting, and who else would be involved.

6. Ask them to consider and discuss this on their own, and to check back with you in a few days if they are interested. Pray during this waiting period, and maintain a natural relationship with them. Don't show an overly serious attitude toward them.

Making the following points can help you persuade people to want to be in your study group.

• This study group can help toward a more stable marriage and family.

• You are a real person—not a "religious freak."

• Christianity can be practical and helpful.

• The Bible is interesting and exciting, especially in today's world.

• This group can help a person learn much about what God is like.

• The Bible teaches principles that work in everyday life.

Orientation
It often works best to have the study at a different home each week if possible. This will evenly distribute the responsibility for refreshments and other preparations.

It may be best to have one of the first sessions in the home of someone who might otherwise be less likely to attend. Another consideration is to have it in the home where the most babysitting expense would otherwise be incurred.

No more than one or two other Christians besides yourself should be in the group. And, of course, any Christians who are present should not dominate the discussion, or react with surprise or criticism to unusual questions and comments made by the non-Christians.

Your first meeting should be for orientation—giving everyone an idea of what he will be doing, and motivating him to want to attend the remaining sessions. The primary goal of this first meeting is to promote a warm and comfortable feeling in the group.

Some members of the group may have brought along some friends you haven't met. Be sure to get acquainted with them, and include them in the discussion.

As you begin, have each person tell something about himself, such as his name, where he grew up, and his vocation. Share this information about yourself first.

It may be helpful to have Bibles on hand for those who may not have brought one. Show them the table of contents, and explain the location and general organization of both Old and New Testaments. Show them how to read a Bible reference and how to find chapters and verses.

Distribute copies of any study material you plan to use, and work through some of it together. Give the group plenty of time to think about the questions that are asked, and then discuss together their answers.

As you explain what you will be doing in your next meeting, mention these points:

• In question-and-answer Bible study material where they will be writing in their answers, they should feel free to leave anything blank which they don't understand. The group can answer it together at your next meeting.

• Each person should do his own work, rather than couples filling out the material together.

• For the purpose of this study and your discussion, ask if everyone would agree at least temporarily to accept two assumptions: (1) that there is a God, and (2) that the Bible's teachings are true and authoritative.

• Ask everyone to try not to miss any sessions, since you will only be having a few. This will make the discussions better.

Make sure you maintain a warm and friendly atmosphere throughout this first session. Normally there should be some simple refreshments afterward, and during this time it may be best to talk about something other than the Bible and Christianity, unless someone brings this up. Try to talk about what they are most interested in in their daily lives. Concentrate on personable, friendly conversation.

As the group members leave, let them know that you enjoyed being with them and that you look forward to seeing them again.

Communication

The remaining sessions after the first one should be designed to effectively communicate the essentials of the gospel to your group. The Bible study material you choose for the group should include this information.

Follow these guidelines:

1. Remember that a home is usually the best location. Non-Christians often are not comfortable in a church.

2. Each week begin with time for greetings and friendly conversation. This could last about fifteen minutes.

3. Each session should last no longer than an hour.

4. If you are leading the discussion as a couple, it may be helpful for the husband to sit on one side of the room and his wife on the other. This could give you a better chance of observing the group's reactions throughout the discussion. Don't do it if, however, it seems unusual to the others.

5. Find out how much work the group members were able to do on their study preparation for the week. Also, make Bibles available to anyone who didn't bring one.

6. If the group is not prepared, try one of these approaches:

• Prepare and discuss together in the group one question at a time.

• Take a few moments to write answers for some of the questions silently and individually, and then discuss them.

• Assign certain questions to each person there. Let them all work silently, then discuss each question together.

Remember that your main objective is to ensure that during the group discussion the material is clearly and thoroughly communicated. Each group member should understand what the Bible teaches on the subjects you study.

Confrontation

If you have created a relaxed and open atmosphere in the study group, made each person feel that you are a friend, and communicated the gospel clearly, then confronting them about receiving Christ as Savior can occur without causing tension or frustration. It will come naturally and comfortably.

In an investigative Bible study group, this confrontation can take place in your last session together. If you feel that each non-Christian in the group is ready to believe in Christ, you would probably want to handle the confrontation in the group meeting. If some are ready and some are not, you may want to meet at another time with those who are ready, and give them an opportunity to individually make their decision for Christ.

Asking questions such as these can help you evaluate their readiness: "What has been your reaction to our discussions together?" "Have our discussions been interesting?" "Have they been helpful?" "How do you feel about them?"

Let the members talk freely about how they feel. This will help you understand where each of them is spiritually. You may spot one or two who don't clearly understand the gospel. Others may have come to Christ on their own.

If you decide to confront them all together, you might say something like this:

"Thank you for sharing all of your thoughts. It sounds as though this has been a worthwhile time for all of us. My wife and I have really enjoyed being with you.

"In just a couple of minutes I would like for all of us to pray aloud together. I will say a sentence and you can repeat it after me. Maybe some of you are sure you have received Christ and have eternal life. Some of you think so, but aren't sure. Some of you may be sure you have never received Christ, and now you want to. Whatever category you feel you are in, we can still pray this prayer sincerely together from the depths of our hearts.

"These are the basic contents of the gospel which we have studied together:
• that we have all sinned and separated ourselves from God;
• that the penalty for what we have done wrong is eternal death;
• that Christ died so we could be free from this penalty;
• that Christ rose from the dead, and we can personally invite Christ into our lives now in order to receive the gift of his life within us.

"After all of our discussion on these issues, are there any further questions or comments that any of you would like to make before we pray? What do you think about these issues? Do you believe all of these things?"

Pause here and let them comment. You may want to then read over the content of the prayer to see if they all agree with its content. Some may prefer to pray these things silently, or on their own at a later time. Be sure to respect their feelings.

Here is an example of the prayer you could then pray, and how you would introduce it:

"In a moment we'll bow our heads. I'll say a sentence or a phrase and you can each repeat it aloud together after me. Then I'll say another sentence and you can repeat it, and so on through the prayer. If you can't sincerely pray these things right now, please feel free to remain silent.

"Let's bow our heads.

'Heavenly Father, I thank you for your great love for me. I thank you that your Son Jesus went through so much suffering for me! I'm grateful for your love.

'I know I have done things wrong which have hurt and displeased you. I know I have tended to neglect you and stray from you.

'I also know that the penalty for my sin is eternal death. I know that you are a completely holy and perfect God. I know I need forgiveness for what I have done.

'I thank you that Jesus died on the cross so that I can be free from the penalty for my sins.

'Right now, Lord, I invite you to come into my heart through your Son Jesus Christ, if you never have before. I want to be sure you are in my life. Give me now the gift of eternal life as you have promised.

All these things I pray with sincerity, from my heart, and with thanksgiving for your love for me. I pray in Jesus' name. Amen.'"

After this prayer, you can help them have assurance of salvation by reviewing a passage such as 1 John 5:11-12 with them. Don't try to drill this assurance into them, however. Provide them with the clear scriptural evidence, and pray in the coming days that the Holy Spirit will give them assurance of their new relationship with God.